W9-BZN-252

THE PEOPLES OF NORTH AMERICA
BEFORE COLUMBUS

LOOKING BACK

THE PEOPLES OF
NORTH
AMERICA
BEFORE COLUMBUS

CHRISTINE HATT

RSVP

**RAINTREE
STECK-VAUGHN**
P U B L I S H E R S
A Steck-Vaughn Company

Austin, Texas

Editors: Nicola Barber, Shirley Shalit, Pam Wells
Designer: Neil Sayer
Picture research: Victoria Brooker
Maps: Nick Hawken
Production: Jenny Mulvanny

Consultant: Dr. Karen Harvey, Associate Dean, University College, University of Denver

Library of Congress Cataloging-in- Publication Data

Hatt, Christine.
    The peoples of North America before Columbus / Christine HAtt.
        p.   cm. — (Looking back)
    Includes bibliographical references and index.
    Summary: Examines the life styles, forms of government, and spiritual beliefs of the people who inhabited North America up to the sixteenth century and looks briefly at the impact of colonization.
        ISBN 0–8172–5426–9
        1. Indians of North America — History — Juvenile literature.
    2. Indians of North America — Social life and customs — Juvenile literature. [1. Indians of North America]   I. Title.   II. Series.
    E77.4.H375   1999
    970.01'1 — dc 21   98-6037
                                                         CIP   AC

Printed in Spain
Bound in the United States
1 2 3 4 5 6 7 8 9 0   01 00 99 98

Acknowledgments

Cover (main image) Werner Forman Archive (background) Eye Ubiquitous **Title page** Seattle Art Museum, Gift of John H. Hauberg/Paul Macapia **page 7** (left) Stephen J Krasemann/Bruce Coleman Limited (right) Mr Jules Cowan/Bruce Coleman Limited **page 9** British Museum/Bridgeman Art Library **page 12** (left) Werner Forman Archive (right) British Museum **page 13** Utah Museum of Natural History **page 14** Salamander Picture Library **page 15** © 1996 Comstock, Inc **page 16** (top and bottom) Werner Forman Archive **page 17** Werner Forman Archive **page 18** Werner Forman Archive **page 20** (top) Werner Forman Archive (bottom) A.J.G. Bell/Eye Ubiquitous **page 21** Richard A. Cooke/Corbis **page 22** Lynton Gardiner/© American Museum of Natural History **page 24** Peter Newark's Pictures **page 25** (top) Werner Forman Archive (bottom) Werner Forman Archive **page 27** Werner Forman Archive **page 29** Library of Congress/Corbis **page 30** Gunter Marx/Corbis **page 31** (top) Peter Newark's Western Americana (bottom) Lynton Gardiner/© American Museum of Natural History **page 32** Museum of History and Industry/Corbis **page 33** Library of Congress/Corbis **page 34** Werner Forman Archive **page 35** Peter Newark's Western Americana **page 36** Michael Maslan Historic Photographs/Corbis **page 37** The National Archives/Corbis **page 38** Phil Shermeister/© Corbis **page 39** Lynton Gardiner/© American Museum of Natural History **page 40** Michael Maslan Historic Photographs/Corbis **page 41** Peter Newark's Western Americana **page 42** Peter Newark's American Pictures **page 43** L. Johnstone/Eye Ubiquitous **page 44** Seattle Art Museum, Gift of John H. Hauberg/Paul Macapia **page 46** Peter Newark's American Pictures **page 47** David Muench/Corbis **page 48** British Museum/Bridgeman Art Library **page 49** (top) Lynton Gardiner/© American Museum of Natural History (bottom) E. O. Hoppé/Corbis **page 51** Werner Forman Archive **page 52** Werner Forman Archive **page 53** Salamander Picture Library **page 54** (bottom) Werner Forman Archive **page 55** Peter Newark's American Pictures **page 57** Werner Forman Archive **page 59** Barry Davies/Eye Ubiquitous

CONTENTS

INTRODUCTION

This book tells the story of the people who inhabited North America before the arrival of Europeans in the 16th century. It explains how people first reached North America many thousands of years ago, and how they gradually spread far and wide across the continent. It examines the extraordinary variety of lifestyles and forms of government they developed, as well as their complex spiritual beliefs. Finally, it looks briefly at the devastating impact of European arrival and colonization on the native population up to 1700 and beyond.

A CLOSER LOOK

When the Italian explorer, Christopher Columbus, set sail from Spain in 1492, he was not looking for the Americas. In fact, he did not even know they existed. His aim was to find an ocean route to Asia, since the Portuguese controlled the trade routes around Africa, and the overland journey from Europe to the East was long and dangerous. Columbus called his mission the "Enterprise of the Indies," because one of the destinations he hoped to reach was India. When Columbus first arrived in the Americas, he assumed that he had achieved his goal. So he called the native peoples that he encountered "Indians," but today they are more accurately known as Native Americans or American Indians. Columbus's voyages marked the beginning of European contact with the peoples of the Americas, and of the continent's transformation.

ENVIRONMENTS AND LIFESTYLES

North America is a huge landmass, covering about 9 million square miles (23.5 million sq km). Within this vast area there are many different landscapes, from the frozen wastes of the Arctic north to the dry, dusty deserts of the southwest. When Europeans arrived, it is estimated that there were roughly seven million people living in North America, divided into more than 300 tribes. Each tribe had its own unique way of life, which depended largely on its particular environment.

To help them study and understand the Native Americans of North America, anthropologists have divided the continent into ten culture areas (see map

Native Americans made – and continue to make – their homes in places as diverse as icy Baffin Island, Canada (left), and the arid deserts of Arizona, southwestern U.S. (below).

on page 8). These are regions whose natural features (for example rivers, forests, or mountains), climate, animals, and plants greatly influenced the lifestyles of their Native American inhabitants. Within each culture area, many tribes shared food-finding methods, and often used the same locally available materials for building their homes.

Tribes within an area often differed from one another in important ways, too. In many areas, some tribes were nomadic, while others lived in permanent villages and towns. On the fringes of each area, tribes often had "mixed" lifestyles. These included customs and practices that were typical of the neighboring area, as well as of their own.

LANGUAGE FAMILIES

Between them, 15th-century North Americans spoke more than 200 languages – perhaps as many as 600. Anthropologists have used these as another way of

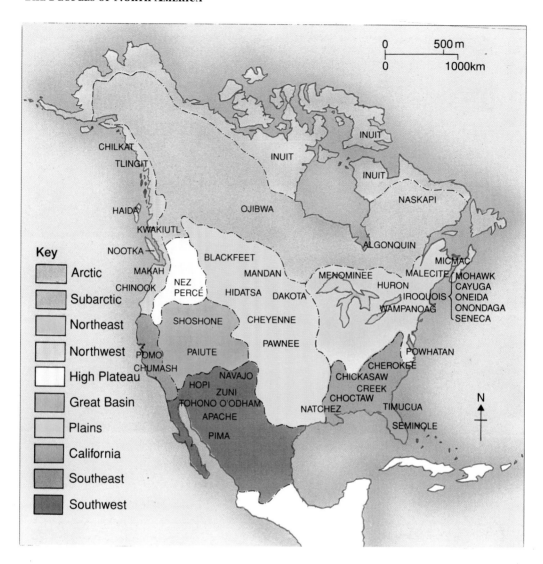

0 500 m

0 1000 km

Key

Arctic

Subarctic

Northeast

Northwest

High Plateau

Great Basin

Plains

California

Southeast

Southwest

This map shows the ten culture areas into which modern anthropologists divide the North American continent. (Tribes shown here are those mentioned in the book.)

dividing the tribes into groups for study, but language divisions have proved much harder to define than culture areas. This is partly because there is not enough evidence – none of the Native American languages of North America had a written form. However, most experts now agree that between 21 and 30 language families, groups of related languages, existed in North America at the time of European contact.

HOW DO WE KNOW?

The tribes of ancient North America kept no written records of any kind. This lack of written evidence has

The manner of their attire and painting them felues when they goe to their generall huntings, or at theire Solemne feasts.

During the late 16th century, English explorer John White spent some time in the southeastern U.S. A talented artist, he compiled a sketchbook of the local Native Americans, including this image of a young warrior.

hampered historians' efforts to piece together an accurate picture of life before the arrival of Europeans. But fortunately, other sources of information are available. Archaeologists working in many parts of the continent have unearthed a huge variety of objects, including tools, weapons, pottery, animal bones, and food preparation equipment, such as stones for grinding seeds.

In some major archaeological sites, hundreds of objects have been discovered. In ancient burial grounds of the eastern woodlands, for example, there are human remains, and grave goods, such as bracelets and pipes. In the buffalo and mammoth kill sites of the plains, there are mounds of animal bones, as well as weapons, and tools for carving meat from carcasses.

The lack of written evidence has forced historians to turn to the accounts of the first European explorers and settlers in North America for information about early Native American life.

But they treat these sources with caution. Most Europeans of the period did not speak Native American languages, although they sometimes tried to communicate using sign language. As a result, they had little understanding of Native American ideas and beliefs, but simply recorded their assumptions as facts. Some Europeans were prejudiced against Native Americans, believing them to be uneducated savages. Others saw them only as slaves, potential converts to Christianity, or sources of valuable trade goods. For all these reasons, 15th- and 16th-century European sources are often unreliable.

ARRIVAL AND SETTLEMENT

The landbridge that emerged between Siberia and Alaska during the last Ice Age allowed people to walk from Asia to North America. Avoiding the massive ice sheets that covered much of the continent, they then made their way south.

The first people ever to set foot on North American soil arrived toward the end of the last Ice Age. At that time, so much of the world's water was frozen that the sea level fell by about 330 feet (100 m). As a result, large areas of land emerged from beneath the waves. In the Far North, newly revealed land formed a bridge between Siberia in Asia, and Alaska in North America. This 994 mile-(1600-km) wide landbridge, known as Beringia, provided the route for the earliest migrations into the Americas.

The first migrants from Asia did not set out to reach North America. They were simply bands of

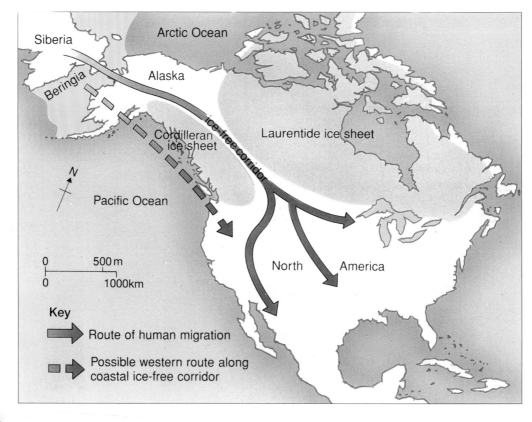

Siberia

Arctic Ocean

Alaska

Beringia

Cordilleran ice sheet

ice-free corridor

Laurentide ice sheet

Pacific Ocean

N

0   500 m
0   1000km

North   America

Key

➡ Route of human migration

⬛➡ Possible western route along coastal ice-free corridor

A CLOSER LOOK

Painstaking archaeological research has revealed much about the origins of the first North Americans. But each Native American tribe has its own stories about how the world was created. These stories express the close links with the natural world that characterized early Native American societies. The creation story of the Taos Pueblo people of the Southwest says that giants once lived in the world. A dreadful disease killed them all except for one boy, but he was bitten by a poisonous snake. He wept at his fate, bled from his wound, and died. His tears turned into lakes, his blood into the red soil of the deserts, and his lifeless body into mountains. And so the Earth was formed.

hunters who followed their prey of giant buffalo, mammoths, mastodons, and other big game across Beringia and unknowingly entered a different continent. Then, they gradually spread south, making their way along an ice-free corridor between the two vast ice sheets that covered much of the land. Some experts believe that there was a second ice-free route far to the west, but this has yet to be proven.

A QUESTION OF TIME

Most experts agree that this was *how* people came to the Americas. But there are many opinions about exactly *when* they made their journeys. Beringia first emerged about 60,000 years ago, then disappeared and reappeared from time to time over the next 50,000 years, as the sea level rose and fell. To find out when people crossed this landbridge, archaeologists have measured the age of the most ancient campsites and tools in the Americas, using radiocarbon dating. The results are confusing. In Alaska, where the migrants probably arrived first, objects about 12,000 years old have been found. Farther to the south, objects dating back about 14,000 years have been discovered. Even more strangely, in South America, far from Beringia, objects over 30,000 years old have been unearthed. The experts are still searching for more conclusive evidence. For now, they can only estimate that the peopling of the Americas occurred over many thousands of years, some time between 40,000 and 12,000 years ago.

THE PALEO-INDIAN PERIOD

Archaeologists call the era of American history that lasted from the time of the first human settlements

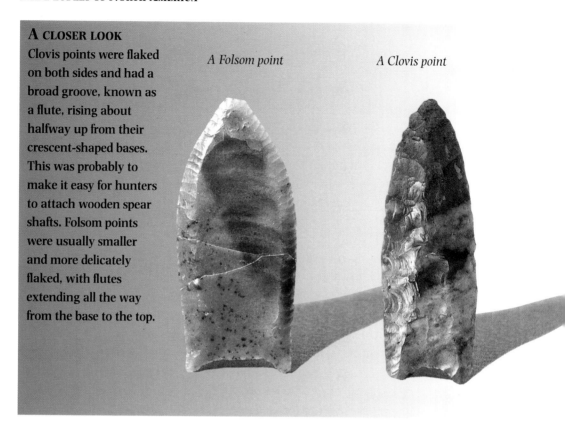

A CLOSER LOOK
Clovis points were flaked on both sides and had a broad groove, known as a flute, rising about halfway up from their crescent-shaped bases. This was probably to make it easy for hunters to attach wooden spear shafts. Folsom points were usually smaller and more delicately flaked, with flutes extending all the way from the base to the top.

A Folsom point

A Clovis point

until about 10,000 years ago the Paleo-Indian, or "ancient Indian" Period. Paleo-Indians are divided into cultures according to the type of stone tools they made. One of the most widespread was the Clovis culture, which lasted from about 10,000 to 9200 B.C. It was named after Clovis, New Mexico. The people of the Clovis culture were nomadic hunters who lived on animals such as tapirs, small prehistoric horses, buffalo, and mammoths. They killed and cut up their prey with Clovis points – spearheads and other tools produced by chipping flakes from pieces of flint. A slightly later Paleo-Indian culture was the Folsom culture. Its members were big game hunters, too, but their main prey was buffalo.

Although all Paleo-Indians were big game hunters, they probably also ate plant foods, such as berries, fruits, and nuts. This method of obtaining food is called hunting and gathering, and it was used by early peoples not just in North America but all over the world.

THE ARCHAIC PERIOD

About 11,000 years ago, the Ice Age began to come to an end, the giant glaciers started to melt and temperatures gradually rose. This process of warming brought great changes to North America. First, the landscape altered. The band of evergreen forests and wide, treeless tundra that had covered the center of the continent moved northward with the ice. In its place, vast open grasslands, dry plains, and deciduous forests appeared. At the same time, mammoths, mastodons, and many other Ice Age mammals died out, probably as a result of the loss of their icy habitats.

The transformation of the landscape and climate made it essential for early North Americans to alter their way of life and adapt to the changing environment. They became less reliant on big game hunting and adopted a more varied range of hunter-gatherer lifestyles from about 8000 B.C. This marked the beginning of the Archaic Period.

Archaic Indians spread across North America, settling in many regions that had previously been too inhospitable. Once they had chosen their territory, many became less nomadic. Some groups evolved a yearly route around a few fixed sites, such as lakesides or caves, while a few even settled in one area. This was only possible where food supplies were abundant.

Many objects from the Archaic Period have been unearthed in Danger Cave, which is located high above the Great Salt Lake in Utah. They include the remains of baskets and nets, besides bone tools and stone spearheads like this one.

For example on the Northwest Coast, fish, seabirds, berries, and nuts were always available.

The Archaic Period came to an end when North Americans began to cultivate their own food – in other words, to farm. In some areas, such as the Northeast, this happened in about 1000 B.C. But in others, such as the Northwest, people continued to hunt animals and gather plant foods until Europeans arrived and transformed their ancient ways of life.

A CLOSER LOOK

As they adapted their skills to the new conditions, Archaic Indians produced many new tools and weapons. Unlike the Paleo-Indians, who all used very similar implements, each Archaic group designed tools suitable for its own specific needs. In the Northeast woodlands, for example, people designed tools for hollowing out tree trunks to make canoes. Archaic tools were also made with a much wider range of materials, including copper, bone, and clay, as well as stone.

EARLY CULTURES

Early North Americans cultivated gourds and squash for their seeds and flesh, and some species of sunflower for their oil-filled seeds. Another type of sunflower was grown for its underground tubers, or underground stems, (below). In English, these tubers are Jerusalem artichokes, a strange name that comes from the Italian word for sunflower, *girasole*.

The peoples of the North American cultures that emerged at the end of the Archaic Period grew crops such as gourds, squash, and sunflowers (see box). At first, these foods made up only a minor part of their diet, which still largely consisted of meat, fish, wild berries, nuts, and roots. But, as Native Americans' farming skills improved, cultivated crops gradually became more important. Besides eating these foods as soon as they were harvested, people also learned to store them. This allowed them to survive in times of drought, when wild plant foods and animals were not available.

Some Native Americans did not become farmers. In some places, such as along the Northwest Coast, people continued their lives as hunters and gatherers, relying on the plentiful supplies of wild food in these areas (see page 13).

THE ADENA CULTURE

The Adena people established one of the earliest cultures of this era that is sometimes known as the Woodland Period. They lived in the Eastern Woodlands of the Ohio River Valley from about 1000 B.C., and left behind archaeological remains in over 200 sites. Many Adena settlements contained huge earthworks, often in the shape of squares or circles. But the most extraordinary of these

The extraordinary Great Serpent Mound in Ohio was first excavated in 1885. Many modern archaeologists think that it was built by the Adena people. Others believe that its impressive size and construction mark it out as the work of the more ambitious Hopewell (see page 16).

structures, the 712-foot-long (217-m) Great Serpent Mound in Adams County, Ohio, takes the form of a giant snake. Experts believe that the Adena earthworks were probably used for religious rituals.

Many Adena villages had a second distinctive feature — massive earth burial mounds up to 65 feet (20 m) high. The graves underneath these cone- and dome-shaped mounds were of two main types. Simple clay basins contained the cremated remains of ordinary people. More elaborate log tombs were the final resting places of the wealthy. The difference between the tombs of rich and poor shows that, unlike the earliest Americans, the Adena had developed a form of hierarchical society, made up of different social classes, probably ruled by clan chiefs.

The grave goods found inside these tombs have provided archaeologists with a great deal of evidence about the Adena way of life. Bracelets and spoons made of copper from Michigan, and beads made of shells from southern coasts, prove that the Adena had trade links with Native Americans in other parts of the continent. Tube-shaped pipes suggest that they grew and smoked tobacco, probably as part of religious ceremonies.

THE HOPEWELL CULTURE

In about 300 B.C., the Hopewell mound-building culture replaced the Adena in Ohio, then spread out in every direction. The Hopewell cultivated corn as well as the sunflowers and other crops of the Adena. At the same time, they continued to hunt game and gather the abundant wild plant foods in the region. This combination of agriculture, hunting, and gathering led to an increase in population.

This vicious-looking bird claw was cut from mica by an artist of the Hopewell culture.

Everything the Adena had done, the Hopewell did on a grander scale. They constructed huge earthworks, some of which covered an area of 100 acres (40 ha). These structures were probably ceremonial centers where sacred rituals were carried out. High banks enclosed the earthworks and inside were numerous burial mounds, in addition to the homes of religious leaders and the ruling clan chiefs. Outside were the farms of ordinary people, who lived in wigwams.

Excavations in the Hopewell tombs have unearthed a dazzling array of grave goods. They include jewelry, shapes cut from sheets of mica (a transparent mineral), carved

A CLOSER LOOK

Many other North American cultures were slowly evolving as those in the East and Southwest emerged. In the eastern Arctic, the Dorset culture arose in about 1000 B.C. Its people made harpoons to catch walrus and seals and built igloos and kayaks. In about A.D. 1000, the Thule culture developed in Alaska and spread east, finally taking over the Dorset people. The Thule were the ancestors of today's Inuit.

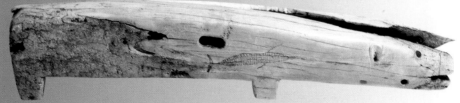

A bone-handled knife, made by a member of the Thule culture. The bone has been skillfully carved into the shape of a polar bear. Its head is clearly visible on the right.

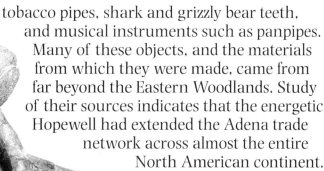

tobacco pipes, shark and grizzly bear teeth, and musical instruments such as panpipes. Many of these objects, and the materials from which they were made, came from far beyond the Eastern Woodlands. Study of their sources indicates that the energetic Hopewell had extended the Adena trade network across almost the entire North American continent. In about A.D. 500, the Hopewell culture began to decline, possibly because of a change in the climate. Whatever the reason, the trading networks gradually broke down, and the Hopewell era came to an end.

The bowl of this Hopewell pipe takes the form of a squat toad. On its back you can see the hole that held the tobacco.

THE MISSISSIPPIANS

Over the next 200 years, different groups of people in the Eastern Woodlands followed their own local ways of life. Then, in about A.D. 700, a powerful new group emerged in the Southeast. The people of this group are known as the Mississippians, because their homelands were in the Mississippi River Valley.

The Mississippians rose to power after they began to cultivate protein-rich beans and a new and highly successful type of corn. At the same time, they learned to use hoes, which made farming easier, and bows and arrows, which improved their hunting skills. All these changes led to increased food supplies, which in turn caused the growth of the population and its expansion into new territories.

The Mississippians built the first towns in North America. A Mississippian town usually had a large square with up to 20 huge, flat-topped mounds around it. On top of the mounds were temples, mortuaries, and sometimes the wooden homes of local chiefs and religious leaders. Ordinary town-dwellers probably lived near the temple mounds in thatched longhouses made of wood and mud plaster. A stockade, a sturdy post and stake fence, often separated the town from the farming villages beyond.

The largest and most powerful Mississippian town was Cahokia, which lay near the Mississippi River. From about A.D. 1050 to 1250, it covered about 5 square miles (13 sq km) and housed some 10,000 people.

In much of the region dominated by the Mississippians, but especially in the south, people followed a religion known as the Southern Cult. Exact details of the cult's beliefs are not known, but death and burial seem to have played a major part in its rituals. Archaeologists have discovered many Southern Cult objects on the temple mounds of Mississippian towns. These include shells and copper sheets carved with designs such as weeping eyes and sunbursts, death masks, and pots in the shapes of human heads.

This Southern Cult gorget (a type of collar worn around the throat) is made of shell and depicts a shaman. He is holding a head in his right hand and a mace in his left.

In the mid-15th century, Cahokia and the other cities of the central Mississippian region fell into decline. This may be because tuberculosis and other diseases spread rapidly, or because farmers could no longer grow enough crops to feed the population. Many city-dwellers moved away and built villages, where they lived in much smaller groups. Some of these people still grew crops, but most returned to older methods of obtaining food — hunting animals and gathering plants.

THE HOHOKAM

Agriculture was introduced to the North American Southwest from present-day Mexico in about 1000 B.C. However, hunting and gathering continued alongside farming for many years, as people slowly learned to grow crops in the dry desert conditions.

The first major culture of the Southwest, the Hohokam, arose some time after 300 B.C. in an area stretching from modern Arizona in the U.S. to Sonora in Mexico. The Hohokam were expert farmers who built irrigation canals to carry river water to their fields. For many years, they lived in pit houses made of twigs, sticks, and clay, a kind of construction known as wattle and daub. These houses were built on rock beneath the desert sands, so only part stood above ground. But in about A.D. 1300, the Hohokam began to construct adobe villages at ground level. The shelters, made of sun-dried mud and straw, were often surrounded by high defensive walls.

In the mid-15th century there was a farming crisis in Hohokam lands, and food shortages followed. At about the same time, aggressive Apache warriors probably began to attack Hohokam towns and villages. Gradually people left their homelands to settle elsewhere in the region.

THE MOGOLLON

The Mogollon culture emerged on the border of present-day Arizona and New Mexico, to the east of Hohokam lands, in about the 3rd century A.D. By about 600 years later, its people had spread far to the east and built pit-house villages near many rivers in their territory. From about A.D. 1000, they began to live in larger houses, which had their main rooms above ground. Beneath these rooms were under-ground kivas, where men carried out religious rituals (see page 22).

Like the Hohokam, the Mogollon were corn, squash, and cotton farmers, but they did not irrigate their land. Instead, they relied on rainfall and river floods to water their crops. Agriculture alone could not provide sufficient food for the whole population, so throughout the Mogollon period, people continued to hunt animals and gather wild plant foods.

The best-known Mogollon group is the Mimbres, so called because its members lived in the valley of the Mimbres River. From about A.D. 750 to 1250, they produced fine white pottery with geometric designs, people and animals painted in black on its surface. When the owner of a Mimbres pot died, a hole was made in the bowl or plate to "kill" the figures painted on it. It was then placed in the owner's grave or tomb as an offering.

The Mogollon culture died out during the 14th century, probably as a result of drought and crop shortages caused by changes in the climate.

This Mimbres pot is decorated with two human figures. The Mimbres people believed that the figures' spirits would fly out of the hole made in the pot after its owner's death.

THE ANASAZI

The greatest of the early Southwest cultures began to take shape in about 200 B.C., in the region where the boundaries of present-day Utah, Colorado, Arizona, and New Mexico meet. The people who lived there are known as the Basketmakers because they made baskets rather than pots. At first, the Basketmakers depended largely on hunting and

A CLOSER LOOK

In Southwest sites, archaeologists often use a technique known as dendrochronology (tree-ring dating) to work out the age of finds. Dendrochronology was invented in 1914 by the American astronomer Andrew Ellicott Douglass. A new ring of wood grows in tree trunks every year, but the spacing between rings varies according to whether the growing season is dry or wet. By counting the growth rings of newly cut trees to work out their age, then matching the ring patterns to samples of ancient timber, experts can date sites accurately. Dendrochronology is used for wood up to 8,000 years old.

One of the most striking cliffside structures of the Anasazi culture was the Cliff Palace in Mesa Verde, Colorado.

gathering to provide themselves with food, but cultivation of corn and other crops slowly became more important.

By about A.D. 700, the powerful Anasazi culture had developed from the Basketmaker tradition. The Anasazi lived in pit houses that were almost entirely underground, protected from the extreme temperatures of the desert. Their development of complex irrigation systems and of long-rooted plants that could reach water under the dry soil, allowed them to grow crops successfully in these conditions, too. As agriculture flourished, the population grew and spread.

Even before it reached its height in about A.D. 900, the Anasazi culture had begun to change. Multistory apartment houses built high on cliff tops had started to replace the sunken pit houses, while underground kivas were built for ceremonial use. From about 1100, new apartment houses were cut into the cliffs, where they could more easily be defended from attack.

Even more spectacular than the cliff villages were the timber-framed towns in Chaco Canyon, New Mexico. From about A.D. 900, these formed the religious, economic, and cultural centers of the Anasazi lands. Thousands of people lived there, and many more visited from Mexico to trade goods such as turquoise and parrot feathers. The Anasazi abandoned their towns and villages early in the 14th century. As is often the case, the reasons for this development are unclear.

A CLOSER LOOK

The greatest of the Chaco Canyon towns was Pueblo Bonito, whose tiered apartment houses were constructed in a D-shape around a huge amphitheater. These houses contained about 800 rooms and were home to about 1,200 people.

THE WORLD OF THE SPIRITS

Each of the North American tribes that inhabited the continent until the arrival of Europeans had its own distinctive lifestyle. But they all shared a profound belief in a spirit world that influenced human thoughts and actions, and that could in turn be influenced by them.

KIVAS AND KACHINAS

The Pueblo peoples of the Southwest – the Pima, Tohono O'odham, Zuni, and Hopi – evolved a complex system of religious beliefs that governed every aspect of their lives. All-male religious societies ensured that the annual round of sacred ceremonies was correctly carried out. The aim of these ceremonies was to please the spirits so that they would enable people to live in harmony with the natural world.

The secret rites of the religious societies were held in underground kivas. Dramatic public ceremonies were held outside, led by a man called the *cacique*. In these rituals, men used masks and costumes to impersonate kachinas, the spirits of ancestors,

The Zuni, Hopi, and other Pueblo peoples believed in many different kachinas, and it was difficult for children to remember them all. To help them, adults made wooden kachina dolls.

A CLOSER LOOK
Some of the most important public ceremonies in the Southwest were designed to ensure a successful harvest. The Hopi held a pre-harvest festival during which men held snakes in their mouths, then let them slither away across the desert. The snakes' twisting movements were supposed to resemble lightning and so encourage the rainstorms that would help the crops grow.

THE WORLD OF THE SPIRITS

A CLOSER LOOK
A common way for young men to contact the spirits was the vision quest. This involved spending several days alone on a hillside, neither eating nor drinking. At the end of this period of fasting, men often saw a vision in which a spirit gave them details of sacred rituals they had to carry out. If this spirit was in the form of an animal, it became their personal spirit animal, and they painted it on their shields for protection. Objects relating to the animal, such as teeth or feathers, were placed in their medicine bundle — an animal-skin bag that contained items believed to have spiritual power.

animals, or even natural forces, such as thunder or wind. Then they performed sacred dances, during which they themselves became the spirits.

THE GREAT SPIRIT

The Native Americans of the Plains culture area, such as the Dakota, Cheyenne, and Pawnee, believed in one great supernatural power that was present everywhere and influenced everything. The Dakota called it "Waken Tanka," the "Great Spirit." Each tribe had its own stories about the spirit, and its own ceremonies. But all tried to communicate with this powerful but unseen force through both prayer and sacrifice.

The greatest of the religious ceremonies was called the Sun Dance. This ritual took place in high summer and lasted for up to a week. Its aim was to establish harmony within the tribe and between the tribe and the spirits. Before the Sun Dance began, the dancers (all men) purified themselves in medicine lodges. These enclosed, hide-covered structures contained fires on which herbs and water were poured to produce a fragrant steam. Inside, the men sweated impurities from their bodies and cleansed their minds and spirits through prayer. Meanwhile, the Sun Dance enclosure was made ready. The trunk of a cottonwood tree was erected at its center, and a

A CLOSER LOOK
Scattered across the Plains region of North America are stone structures in the shape of large spoked wheels, with small mounds of stones in the center. These medicine wheels may have had several purposes. They were probably a form of calendar, read by measuring the movements of the stars against the fixed positions of the spokes. By consulting them, the Plains tribes may have worked out when to hunt buffalo or hold ceremonies. These wheels are considered sacred.

buffalo skull was placed either on top of the trunk or on an east-facing altar.

Different tribes carried out the Sun Dance in different ways, but a common feature was the dancers' endurance of a painful ordeal. Among the Dakota, this involved piercing each dancer's chest with two skewers and threading strips of hide through the holes. The strips were then attached to the central pole and the dancer leaned back, so that the skewers carried his full weight. He remained in this position all day, following the sun with his eyes from its rising to its setting and offering his suffering to the spirits. In this way, he prayed to bring good fortune to himself and his tribe.

SECRET SOCIETIES AND SHAMANS

About 30 Native American tribes lived in the Northwest culture area, including the Kwakiutl, the Nootka, and the Chilkat. They developed a rich mythology that explained the links between humans and the natural world, and they expressed their beliefs in spectacular rituals and ceremonies.

A Blackfeet Indian participating in the Sun Dance ritual. The Sun Dance was outlawed in 1881, but it became legal again in 1934.

Northwestern tribes believed in a supernatural world that was populated with the spirits of the animals they saw around them every day. Chief among these was Raven, who was both the creator of the world and a trickster, always deceiving unwary humans. Other important animal spirits were those of bears, wolves, salmon, and killer whales. These spirit animals were totems, each one symbolizing a Native American clan or moiety (see page 30). A family acknowledged its totem by carving it into their totem

The Northwestern spirit world contained not only real animals but also mythical creatures, such as the mighty two-headed Thunderbird. This Thunderbird mask was worn by members of the Haida tribe during sacred dances. At certain times during the dance, the beak was opened to reveal the person inside.

poles, wearing images of it on their clothing, and acting out the stories about it. But they did not worship it as a god.

Northwestern tribes communicated with spirits to keep the unpredictable supernatural powers on their side. Adolescents, usually males, attempted to make contact by separating themselves from society for several months. At the end of this period of isolation they received a vision

A CLOSER LOOK

The Northwestern tribes considered sickness to be a sign of spiritual distress, often caused by the soul's escape from the body. So they called on healers, known as shamans, to bring the soul back from the spirit world. Both men and women were shamans. They were believed to have a direct link with the spirits, which they contacted by shaking wooden rattles.

This frightening wooden rattle belonged to a shaman of the Northwestern Haida tribe.

25

of their guardian spirit, and they joined a secret society that carried out its rites. The secret societies of the Northwestern tribes, particularly the Kwakiutl, staged dramatic rituals and dances throughout the winter. Participants wore carved wooden masks and striking costumes to represent the spirits and reenact tribal stories.

FESTIVALS AND FALSE FACES

The Native Americans of the Northeast were dominated by the five main Iroquois tribes—the Mohawk, Cayuga, Oneida, Onondaga, and Seneca—but also included about 40 others. All these tribes had two central beliefs. These were that everything, humans, animals, plants, rivers, even rain, had a spirit, and that all spirits were linked by one great spiritual force. The Iroquois called this force *orenda*, while others knew it as Manitou.

Many people of the Northeastern tribes were farmers, so their spiritual life was closely linked to the cycle of the agricultural year. The Iroquois had six main agricultural festivals. These included the spring Maple Festival, which marked the rising of the sap in the sugar maple trees, and the Green Corn Festival, which marked the ripening of the "three sisters," their three main crops of corn, beans, and squash. But the most important was the seven-day Midwinter Festival. This was held at the beginning of February, the time of the Iroquois New Year, and was a period of cleansing and renewal. The most important participants were members of the Husk Face Society, who wore corn

A CLOSER LOOK
The life of the Arctic Inuit people revolved around the sea, and the whales, seals, and other food animals that it provided. The Inuit believed that a powerful female spirit, often known as Sedna, lived under the sea. She was believed to control the lives of all its creatures, including their mysterious seasonal migrations, and also to be responsible for whipping up savage ocean storms. Inuit shamans contacted Sedna by going into a trance. When they emerged, they proclaimed the spirit's message in song. It often consisted of advice about where to find good fishing grounds.

A wooden mask used by an Iroquois False Face Society. The grotesque appearance of such masks was intended to drive away evil spirits.

husk masks. Their role was to persuade the spirits to provide a good harvest in the coming year, and to grant the birth of many healthy babies.

The Iroquois also formed societies of healers. These were known as False Face Societies, because their members wore masks carved from the trunks of living trees. If an individual became ill, the healers performed dances designed to cure the sickness. But they also had a duty to prevent disease in the wider community. So twice a year, in autumn and spring, they carried out purification rituals in every longhouse.

SPIRITS OF THE SOUTHEAST

Like their neighbors to the north, Southeastern tribes, such as the Creek, Choctaw, Chickasaw, and Cherokee, believed that there were spirits everywhere around them, but that ruling over all was one supreme spirit, sometimes known as the Great Spirit. They held many ceremonies, including a Green Corn Ceremony similar to that of the Northeast, to communicate with the spirits or to thank them for gifts received. Priests played a central role throughout the region, relaying messages between people and spirits. They also healed the sick, often with the aid of plant remedies.

GOVERNMENT AND SOCIETY

Native American tribes governed themselves in many different ways, although tribes within the same culture area often had similar forms of government. Society was organized in many ways, too, with the roles of men, women, and children, and the relationships between them, varying from one area to another. Social organization was closely linked to the tribe's physical environment. Complex societies could evolve only when the climate and availability of food guaranteed basic survival.

LIFE IN THE PUEBLOS

In the bustling pueblos of the Southwest, the Zuni, Hopi, and other peoples lived in multifamily groups inside multistory apartment houses. The dry desert climate often caused crop failures, while the Navajo and Apache tribes were a constant threat. To survive in this hostile environment, pueblo families had to cooperate closely. So they developed organized governments and well-ordered societies.

Each pueblo had its own rules, but many were governed in the same way. A pueblo's ruling council was made up of tribal elders. These men were usually either the leaders of religious societies (see pages 22-23) or the chiefs of large family groups called clans. The council members met regularly to make decisions about village life and to devise new sets of rules.

Every pueblo family was responsible for both its own welfare and the welfare of the entire village. Each grew its own food but had to save some of its crops. These were stored, then shared equally when the harvest was bad. In the same way, men from

A CLOSER LOOK

A young woman of the Southwestern Hopi tribe prepared herself for marriage by learning household skills, especially corn grinding, from her mother. When she was ready to find a husband, she arranged her hair into two large coils, one on either side of her head. This was known as the squash blossom style (right). Once her partner had been chosen, the mothers of the future bride and groom washed their children's hair together in the same bowl. At the wedding ceremony, the bride wore clothes that had been woven by her husband-to-be and other men of his family. Afterward, the new wife abandoned her squash blossom hairstyle and wore braids instead.

different families grouped together to guard farmers from attack as they worked. Although they could not join religious societies or ruling councils, women had an important place in pueblo life. They owned all family property and passed it on to their daughters when they died.

PLAINS POLITICS

Before contact with Europeans, most Plains tribes were seminomadic. People of these tribes planted a few crops in the spring, hunted buffalo on foot in summer, and then returned to harvest their crops in the autumn. Since they were often on the move, their method of government was informal and flexible. Tribes were made up of several bands of about 100 people, each with one or more chiefs. These men were not all-powerful. If they had to solve a problem, they arranged a meeting with the elders of their band. When this council had come to a decision it was announced, but not enforced.

The roles of men and women in the nomadic Plains tribes were clearly defined. Men were the hunters, while women gathered plant foods and carried out chores such as cooking, cleaning, and preparing rawhides from buffalo skins. Women were also responsible for erecting tepees at new camping sites and taking them down again when it was time to move on. Since the women had so much work to do, many men had several wives.

CLANS AND TOTEMS

The 30 or more tribes that lived in the Northwest culture area were some of the richest Native American peoples. Fish, fruits, and other foods were so plentiful in their homelands that their populations grew quickly. Since it was relatively easy to obtain food, the tribes had spare time to develop fine artwork and complex spiritual beliefs.

The basis of Northwestern society was the family. Families were linked in larger groups known as clans. In some tribes, such as the Tlingit, clans were linked in two larger groups called moieties (halves). Members of the same clan or moiety often lived in different villages or belonged to different tribes. But they always remembered the bond that existed between them. Although marriage between tribes was acceptable, two people of the same clan or moiety were not allowed to become husband and wife.

This strikingly carved totem pole comes from Canada. Many totem poles were free-standing like this. Others formed part of Northwestern houses, providing support for horizontal beams.

Each clan or part of a tribe had its own animal totem (see pages 24-25). The cedarwood poles that towered above Northwestern villages were often carved with several totems. For example, the totem of both a man and his wife might appear on a pole that formed part of their house's framework. Strangers could "read" the poles in a village and immediately tell where to find other members of their clan.

Members of many clans and moieties were divided into three social classes: nobles, commoners, and slaves. Nobles and commoners were usually born into their class, while slaves were often members

The totem poles and houses in this Northwestern Haida village were made from the wood of cedar trees like those in the background.

of other tribes who had been captured during wars. Northwestern nobles were notoriously proud of their high rank. To increase their prestige, they held potlatches. During these ceremonies, people dressed in their finest clothes and feasted for up to 12 days. The main purpose of a potlatch was for the host to demonstrate his importance. He did this by giving away valuable gifts such as wood carvings, copper plaques, and furs. The redistribution of goods that took place during potlatches prevented any one man from becoming too wealthy and upsetting the balance of the community as a whole.

Northwestern nobles wore hats like this whenever they held a potlatch. This particular hat belonged to a member of the Tlingit tribe. The five rings at the top indicate that he had hosted five potlatches.

SOUTHEASTERN SOCIETY

When Spanish explorer Hernando de Soto arrived in the Southeast during the 16th century, he found many chiefs still living on top of huge temple mounds, just as their Mississippian ancestors had done (see page 17). Most tribes, with the notable exception of the Natchez, were governed by these chiefs. The main city of a tribe housed its principal chief. The lesser chiefs, who ruled other towns, regularly sent corn, salt, and other goods to him as tribute. Ordinary people were divided into clans led by women. These women were responsible for the orderly running of community life.

The Natchez were the only tribe ruled by a monarch at the time of European contact. Their ruler was called Quigaltam, meaning the "Great Sun" (see page 33). He was believed to be divine, and had absolute power over his people. His role was hereditary, and it passed not from father to son, but from the ruler's sister to her son.

People of the Natchez tribe carry their ruler, the Great Sun, to a harvest celebration.

NORTHEASTERN SOCIETY

Tribes in the Northeast were divided into clans, each with its own animal symbol, such as a deer, beaver, or wolf. All the members of a clan believed that they were descended from the same ancestors. Marriage was only permitted between a man and a woman of different clans, and a new husband often went to live with his wife's family. If the woman later wanted a divorce, she simply put her husband's possessions outside the door of their multifamily longhouse. Children were named by their mothers, and usually inherited membership of their mother's clan.

The method of government practiced in the Northeast relied on everyone working together for the good of the entire community. Each clan had its own chief. If a decision had to be made that would affect the whole tribe, these men (or occasionally women) met to come to a decision. Any family or clan that disagreed was free to move away.

A CLOSER LOOK

The Iroquois tribes of the Northeast were often at war with one another and with the other major group of tribes in the region, the Algonquians. But during the late 16th century, possibly before contact with Europeans had occurred, the Mohawk, Onondaga, Seneca, Oneida, and Cayuga tribes joined together to form the Iroquois League. This was essentially a political alliance designed to end the violence between them and to strengthen their position in relation to other tribes.

FINDING FOOD

Native Americans obtained food in many ways. In some areas, such as the Northwest, tribes continued the hunter-gatherer lifestyle of the Archaic Period (see page 13) until the arrival of Europeans. In the Southeast, and Northeast, the Southwest, and parts of the Great Plains, naturally available food supplies were supplemented by farmed produce. In barren areas such as the Great Basin, people lived by foraging for plant foods and trapping small animals.

LAND OF PLENTY

The Northwest culture area was like a giant natural pantry, with food almost everywhere. In the Pacific Ocean there were seals, sea lions, and whales. On the shoreline, there was a rich variety of shellfish. Rivers were bursting with salmon, herring, and sardines, as well as the oolakon fish, which provided a delicious oil used in cooking. Men caught these fish with spears, nets, and rakes. They also trapped them behind small dams called weirs. Some of the Northwestern tribes were based too far inland to rely on the sea for food, so people from these tribes hunted bears, elks, and mountain goats.

Throughout the area, women gathered many different plant foods, including blackberries and cranberries. They were also responsible for preparing and cooking food. Meat and fish were often smoked, and fruits were

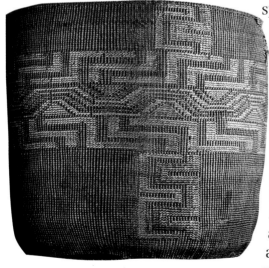

This patterned Tlingit basket was woven from spruce tree roots. Women used it for collecting berries.

A CLOSER LOOK

Men of the Nootka tribe were expert whale hunters. Before setting out, the leader of a Nootka hunting team said prayers to the spirits for success. Then the whalers sped over the Pacific waters in huge, cedarwood canoes, each holding up to ten men. When they got close enough to their prey, they stuck stone-tipped harpoons in its sides. The tips were attached to long lines that remained in the hunters' grasp. As the whales tried to swim away, they pulled the canoes along behind them. Then the whalers waited – sometimes for several days – until the whales died.

A Nootka whale hunter.

dried in the sun, to preserve them for future use. These preserved foods helped the tribe survive the winter.

FOOD FROM THE FREEZER

Finding food in the icy landscapes of the Arctic posed special problems. The lives of the Inuit followed an unchanging seasonal cycle. In winter, they built igloos on the frozen sea, hunted walrus and seals, and fished through holes in the ice with pronged spears. As spring slowly returned, they moved inland to catch lake fish and pick crowberries, sorrel, and other plants. Summer was the time for hunting seals, whales, and other sea mammals in the newly melted coastal waters. The Inuit pursued seals in light canoes called kayaks. To chase larger prey, they preferred bigger sailing boats, known as umiaks. As the summer ended, Inuit tracked lumbering herds of

This umiak set sail from Grantley Harbor in Alaska in about 1904. However, the design of these boats has changed little over the centuries.

caribou and musk oxen as they migrated south for winter, killing them with spears and bows and arrows.

HUNTING THE BUFFALO

Two ways of life existed side-by-side in the Great Plains before the arrival of Europeans. Tribes, such as the Mandan, Hidatsa, and Pawnee, lived in permanent river-valley villages. The women of these tribes were farmers, growing melons and sunflowers as well as corn, beans, and squash. The men were hunters. Other tribes, such as the Blackfeet, were nomadic hunter-gatherers, following buffalo across the Plains all year round and collecting plant foods. Over the centuries, the numbers of these buffalo hunters swelled as other tribes arrived, forced from their homelands by enemy tribes or by Europeans.

The buffalo hunt was central to the Plains way of life. At the beginning of a hunt, shamans often tried to attract the animals by calling to their spirits and waving buffalo-shaped stones called *iniskims*. Then they left the hunters to catch their prey. In the years before Europeans brought horses to the Americas, a common method was to stampede a herd of buffalos over the edge of a cliff, so that the animals fell to their deaths below. Another technique was to put up a corral, then drive the animals into it.

A CLOSER LOOK

Plains women prepared buffalo meat for eating in many ways. They roasted huge joints over fires and used scraps and bones to make stews and soups. Another favorite dish was pemmican. This was made by pounding strips of dried, salted buffalo meat into a powder, then mixing it with melted buffalo fat, dried berries, and sometimes maple syrup. The paste was then rolled into balls, which were sweet, full of energy, and longer-lasting than raw meat.

VARIED DIET

In the Southeast, people were both farmers and hunter-gatherers. A huge variety of crops flourished in the area's fertile lands, but the most important crop was corn. Both men and women worked in the fields, but carried out different tasks. In spring, men turned over the ground with hoes. Women followed behind, planting seeds. In summer, women tended the fields while men went hunting. In autumn, they harvested the crops and took part in the Green Corn ceremony (see page 26).

A CLOSER LOOK

Fishermen from Southeastern tribes did not always rely on their skill with nets and spears alone. Sometimes they drugged fish by putting special herbs into the rivers. Then they simply scooped the dazed creatures up from the surface of the water. The region's rivers and coasts provided the fishermen with other prey, too, including alligators and turtles.

This picture by John White (see page 9) shows Native Americans from North Carolina using many different methods to catch fish.

Agriculture was central to the Southeastern way of life, but hunting and fishing provided over a third of the population's food. Gathering was important, too – wild plant foods, such as strawberries and peanuts, made a major contribution to the varied diet of the Southeastern tribes.

FARMING AND FISHING

In the Northeast, tribes practiced a combination of farming, gathering, and hunting. The major crops were corn, beans, and squash, but sunflowers and tobacco were also grown. Women carried out the bulk of the farm work, but it was the men's duty to prepare the fields for planting in spring by burning down shrubs and trees. Women also gathered fruits, such as blueberries, raspberries, and chokecherries. In the north of the area, around the Great Lakes, the most important wild plant food was wild rice.

The men of the Northeast hunted an amazing range of animals using bows and arrows and clubs. In the forests of southeast Canada, moose, caribou, and bears were important prey for tribes, such as the Micmac and Malecite. The fishing in the Northeast was just as varied as the hunting. In spring, men

Many years ago, members of the Great Lakes tribes harvested wild rice in the early autumn. Sitting or standing in their birchbark canoes, they struck the plant stalks with sticks until the grains fell into their boats. These present-day Indians are using much the same technique.

netted young salmon as the fish hurled themselves up waterfalls toward their spawning grounds. In winter, they made holes in the ice and lowered hooks and lines to catch their prey.

DESERT AGRICULTURE

The Pueblo peoples of the Southwest grew onions, peppers, and tomatoes, as well as corn, squash, and beans. They also bred turkeys. Since the climate was so dry, the tribes developed special techniques to make farming possible. They planted seeds deep in the earth so that they could tap into underground water, and diverted rivers onto the arid soil.

FORAGING FOR FOOD

In the deserts of the Great Basin there was so little rainfall that farming was impossible. Neither was there enough game for people to be full-time hunters, although they occasionally caught a few ducks, deer, and rabbits. Instead they moved around the area foraging for berries, seeds, and nuts, and catching small animals such as grasshoppers, lizards, and prairie dogs.

Duck decoys like this were made from rushes by the Paiute Indians of the Great Basin. Placed on the water, they encouraged real ducks to land. Then the birds were quickly caught by waiting hunters.

Conditions in the more northerly High Plateau area were less harsh. There, the Nez Percé and other tribes were able to catch salmon in the Columbia, Fraser, and Snake rivers, and hunt deer and bighorn sheep. But they also foraged for camas bulbs, roots, and other plant foods. The California culture area was more hospitable still, containing a wide range of environments from forests to coasts. More than 50 tribes lived there, each with its own specialized diet of local foods. However, despite the fertile land in much of the area, agriculture never developed.

39

EVERYDAY LIFE

The housing, clothing, and transportation methods of the many North American tribes were just as varied as their means of finding food. Produced from the different materials available in the different culture areas, they made everyday life in each one distinct from that of its neighbors.

This Inuit couple from Alaska are dressed in fur clothes to keep out the bitter cold of the Arctic.

IGLOOS AND ANORAKS

The clever Inuit learned to make housing, clothing, and canoes from the meager resources available in their frozen lands. Igloos were built on thick sea ice during the winter hunting season (see pages 35-36). They were constructed from blocks of snow sawed out of the ground and shaped with snow knives. In spring and summer the Inuit made houses from other materials. In places where there was a supply of wood, such as Alaska, people used it to make a framework on which to spread animal skins or pieces of sod. Elsewhere, they made their houses from tightly packed sod and stones.

In the Arctic, protective clothing was essential for survival, so the Inuit covered themselves from head to toe in waterproof hooded anoraks, trousers, and boots. The clothes were often made from caribou fur and the boots from sealskin. To shield their eyes from the reflection of the sun off white snow or water, the Inuit also wore wood or walrus-tusk goggles.

The people of the Arctic built lightweight kayaks by making driftwood frames then stretching sealskins across them. Sturdier umiaks (see page 36) were made from wood or whalebone frames covered in walrus hides. Hunters waterproofed both skins and hides by soaking them in seal oil. To travel overland, Inuit used wooden sleds drawn by huskies.

TENTS AND TOBOGGANS

Most subarctic tribes, for example the Ojibwa, lived in wigwams. These were single-family, cone-shaped tents made from a framework of saplings with sheets of birchbark laid over the top. Wigwams were ideal for the tribes' nomadic way of life, since they could be put up and taken down quickly and easily.

Winters in the subarctic were long and severe, so its people wore clothes made of caribou fur. On their feet they wore soft deerskin moccasins, but in the winter they sometimes bound snowshoes over those. These were made from thin strips of caribou

To thank the Great Spirit for the first snowfall of winter, members of the subarctic Ojibwa tribe perform the Snowshoe Dance.

hide woven into a mesh across a birchbark frame. They allowed their wearers to glide across the snow.

The subarctic tribes depended on two main forms of transportation, the birchbark canoe, which they had in common with the Northeastern peoples (see pages 43-44), and the wooden toboggan, which was unique to them. Toboggans were made from planks mounted on curved runners that cut through the snow. The wood of the runners had to be softened in steam before it could be bent into the right shape. The toboggans were usually pulled by men.

BIRCHBARK BUILDERS

Northeastern peoples constructed a variety of houses. Many lived in wigwams, which were either cone- or dome-shaped. Some tribes covered the wooden frames of their wigwams with birch bark, but others used different materials. For example, the Menominee of the Great Lakes used woven mats of reeds.

The other distinctive dwelling of the region was the longhouse, in which the Iroquois and several

These Native Americans erected their birchbark wigwams on the shores of Lake Huron.

other tribes lived. A longhouse was a rectangular structure up to 148 feet (45 m) long. It was made by erecting a framework of wooden poles, tying them together with leather strips, then covering them with bark. Every longhouse was home to as many as 12 families, each of which occupied its own separate compartment, complete with a raised sleeping platform. Food, utensils, and clothes were stored on higher platforms, and a corridor ran down the center where fires were built for cooking. Iroquois villages generally consisted of several, regularly spaced rows of longhouses surrounded by a stockade.

Northeastern tribes paddled around the rivers of their homelands in canoes. These graceful boats were made from sheets of birch bark stretched over cedarwood frames and waterproofed with the

A CLOSER LOOK

The typical clothing of the Northeast was made from the skins of animals, such as deer and moose, sewn together with leather strips. Men wore jackets and leggings in winter and loincloths in summer, while women wore belted, knee-length dresses. Deerskin moccasins were worn on the feet, sometimes in bootlike styles that came almost to the knee. Both clothes and shoes were often decorated with dyed porcupine quills.

This is a reconstruction of a longhouse built by members of the Huron tribe, who lived between Lake Huron and Lake Ontario.

resin of black spruce trees. The river systems of the Northeast were so complex that it was often quicker to cross from one river to another on foot than to make an entire journey by boat. Luckily, birchbark canoes were so light that they could easily be carried by one person.

The most striking garments in the Northwest were made by the Chilkat, a tribe of the Tlingit people. Their ceremonial shirts were woven from cedar bark and goat wool, and covered in designs based on family totems. The totem used in this shirt design is a bear.

LAND OF THE CEDAR

Much of the land along the Northwest Pacific Coast was covered in dense cedar forests. Gigi Northwestern tribes used the water-resistant wood from the trees for their houses. The style of Northwestern houses varied from region to region, but all of them had a fixed inner framework and a portable outer framework that could be replaced if necessary. Cedar was also used for chests, benches, and other furniture inside the houses, and for cooking and storage boxes.

Northwestern tribes made many of their clothes from the bark of the cedar tree. In late spring every year, they pulled long strips of the bark from tree trunks. Then women wove these into clothes — bark blankets for men, bark skirts and cloaks for themselves — on upright looms. Clothes were also made from dog hair, mountain goat wool, and sea otter fur.

Northwestern people used hollowed-out cedar logs to make their main means of transportation— canoes. They built several types. Small, light canoes were made for shallow coastal and river waters, while for long ocean journeys, heavier vessels were constructed from massive tree trunks. Some large canoes were carved and painted with animal designs and used for special occasions, such as weddings and potlatches (see page 31).

TEPEES AND TRAVOIS

The nomadic, hunting tribes of the Great Plains lived in tepees. These were cone-shaped tents made from painted buffalo hides stretched over a frame of pinewood or young willow poles. The lower half of each tepee was lined with a decorated dew cloth to keep it warm and dry inside. A fire for cooking and heating burned in the center, and smoke escaped through a hole in the roof. Family tepees were about 13 feet (4 m) wide, but much larger versions were erected for religious ceremonies and council meetings. All tepees were made and owned by women.

The farming tribes of the Plains lived in dome-shaped earth lodges sunk about three feet (1 m) below ground. These were made from layers of wood, grass, and earth resting on a central framework of tree trunks. From the outside they looked like giant molehills, with only an entranceway and smoke hole revealing the fact that people – and animals – were living inside.

Most Plains clothing was made from deerskin, often decorated with porcupine quills. Everyday garments were similar across the region – loose shirts and leggings for men, straight, loose shifts

The High Plateau tribe known as the Nez Percé became expert horse breeders and traders after the arrival of Europeans. But here they are still using a dog-drawn travois.

(dresses) or skirts for women. However, ceremonial headdresses and robes were more varied. For example, the eagle feather warbonnets of the Dakota hung down their backs to the ground, while those of Blackfeet warriors looked like crowns, with feathers pointing up toward the sky.

The nomadic peoples of the Plains transported their tepees and other goods on wooden frames called travois. A travois was made by joining two pinewood poles at one end to form a triangular shape, then slinging buffalo hides between the poles. Before Europeans arrived, dogs were used to pull travois. Later the bigger, stronger horses took their place.

People of the settled Mandan tribe paddled small bullboats along the rivers of their homelands. They made these boats by creating a cup-shaped framework of flexible willow, then covering it with buffalo skins. Finished boats were gently heated while a mixture of buffalo fat and resin was rubbed into the joints between the hides to seal them.

DESERT DWELLERS

The Pueblo peoples of the Southwest lived in multistory apartment houses made of adobe or stone (see page 21). However, Navajo and Apache homes were completely different. During the summer hunting season, when they moved frequently from place to place, these tribes built temporary shelters from branches and twigs. In the winter they constructed hogans – small, one-roomed structures consisting of cedar log frameworks covered with packed earth. If a person died inside a hogan, a hole was made in the wall to let their spirit out, and the house was never used again.

In the heat of the Southwestern pueblos, there was no need for animal-skin garments. Instead clothes were made from cotton that had been spun and woven into fabric by men. As this cloth was naturally pale, color was often added by applying vivid vegetable dyes. Pueblo women wore long dresses, which they fastened on the right shoulder, while men favored shirts and leggings.

When the Apache and Navajo arrived in the Southwest during the 15th century, they wore skin garments. But they gradually began to barter for cotton clothing from the Pueblos, and to spin and weave for themselves. However, it was not until after the arrival of the Spanish that they became skilled wool weavers. This tradition continues today (see page 53).

This earth-covered hogan is dwarfed by the spectacular scenery of Monument Valley, Arizona.

SOUTHEASTERN STYLE

Houses in the Southeast were quite varied, although most were made from some combination of wood, bark, reeds, and mud. The Natchez lived in domed, wood-framed huts with mud walls and thatched roofs. The Creek made two types of wooden, reed-roofed homes – open-sided summer houses and enclosed winter lodges insulated with clay. In every village they also built a

47

A CLOSER LOOK

The Choctaw and many other Southeastern tribes enjoyed the game of stickball, which is also known as lacrosse. The game was played between two teams, both with hundreds of members. Each member held two sticks with small leather nets at the end, and used the sticks to throw or carry a deerskin ball around a playing field. The aim of the game was to score goals by throwing the ball through posts at either end.

The Southeastern village of Pomeioc, Virginia, was also painted by John White (see page 9). Its houses were made of bark, reeds and wood.

large, circular building, used for council meetings and festivals, and a granary, used for storing corn. The village was often surrounded with a stockade or moat to keep hostile tribes out.

For much of the year, very little clothing was necessary in the humid southern half of the Southeast. Among tribes such as the Timucua of Florida men wore simple loincloths, while women wore short, fringed skirts. These garments were usually made from coarsely woven cotton cloth. In the cooler northern half of the region, leather and fur were the most common clothing materials. But, although clothes in the Southeast were simple, tattooing, jewelry, feather headdresses, and elaborate hairstyles added variety and color to the appearance of the different tribes.

The towne of Pomeiock and true forme of their howses, covered and enclosed some w th matts, and some w th barcks of trees. All compassed about w th smale poles stock thick together in stedd of a wall.

WESTERN WAYS

The tribes of the Great Basin in western North America often lived in caves during the winter. In summer, as they moved around foraging for food, they built wickiups. These were small, cone-shaped dwellings made from a wooden framework covered with a layer of brush. The tribes of the more northerly High Plateau region lived in circular pit houses during winter and in communal reed lodges in summer.

After Europeans arrived in the Great Basin, local tribes developed new types of clothing. This jacket is decorated with European glass beads (see page 54).

Clothes worn in both areas were simple – loincloths for men and apronlike garments for women – and usually made from animal skins or bark from trees.

In general, the Native Americans of the Californian tribes wore little, as the heat of much of the region made clothing unnecessary. Homes were of several types. Some tribes built small wickiups like those in the Great Basin. The coastal Pomo and Chumash tribes constructed thatched houses with wooden frames. But those of the Pomo were long and straight, while those of the Chumash were circular and domed. The Chumash were also remarkable for their boat-building skills. They made sturdy, seagoing canoes from pinewood. Other Californian tribes used reeds to make lighter boats for use on lakes and rivers.

A CLOSER LOOK

In the 18th century, a group of Native Americans from the Southeastern Creek tribe left their homes in the north of the region and went to Florida. These people became the Seminole (meaning "breakaway") tribe. They developed their own unique ways to survive in the swamps and lakes of the Everglades. They lived in chickees—open-sided, thatched houses on stilts—and wore multi-colored cotton clothes. A strong Seminole community of about 14,000 people still exists today, evidence of the tribe's remarkable adaptability through changing times.

These two Seminole girls are wearing the traditional cotton costume of their tribe.

NORTH AMERICAN ARTS

For Native Americans, the ability to create a tool, or weave a garment, was seen as a special and important gift. For this reason, making and using beautiful and practical objects was an integral part of everyday life. It was one of the many ways in which they expressed their links with the world of the spirits and offered thanks to their gods. They generally worked with locally available materials, but trade networks, especially in the Southwest and Northwest, sometimes made it possible to use metals, shells, and stones imported from elsewhere.

ARCTIC ART

The Inuit people were expert carvers of walrus ivory, wood, and stone. Among the objects they most commonly produced were tiny carved figures, many of which have been unearthed in ancient Inuit sites. The exact purpose of these figures is unknown, but they may be charms used by shamans when they tried to contact Sedna (see page 26) and other gods.

The tribes of the subarctic made ceremonial masks, some of them adorned with caribou fur. People of these tribes took great pride in the decoration of their clothes. Some used porcupine quills to create their designs, but the Naskapi tribe were famous for the red patterns they painted on their fur and skin garments.

A CLOSER LOOK

The Inuit carved elaborate masks, some with moving parts, for use in dances and spiritual ceremonies. These usually represented spirits or animals whose behavior they hoped to influence through their rituals. Only men put on the full-size masks, while women wore miniature versions on their fingers. The Inuit also made a wide variety of everyday items, from canoe paddles to sun hats, which were carved or painted with ornate designs.

BASKETS, BOARDS, AND BELTS

Not only did the Northeastern tribes use birch bark for wigwams and canoes, they also wove strips of this light, flexible material into baskets and boxes. These were often decorated with quills. Wood was carved to make other everyday objects, such as bowls, spoons, and cradleboards for carrying babies.

The most distinctive objects made by the Iroquois tribes of the Northeast were wampum belts. These were long, broad bands of black, white, and purple beads (wampum) made from whelk (sea snails) and clam shells. People gave one another gifts of wampum belts to mark important occasions such as marriages or peace agreements. They were sacred objects and extremely valuable. Their patterns recorded important events from a tribe's history, and some men, known as Keepers of the Wampum, were specially trained to interpret them and recount the stories they told.

This beautifully shaped hat, decorated with a mountain goat crest, was woven from spruce tree roots by a member of the Haida tribe.

WOODWORK AND WEAVING

The people of the Northwestern tribes were skilled at carving and painting the wooden totem poles that stood in their villages and the masks that they wore at religious ceremonies (see pages 24-25). They also carved a wide range of everyday objects, such as bowls, from other materials, including stone, bone, antlers, and the twisted horns of mountain sheep. Many of the Northwestern peoples were expert weavers. Each of the bark and hair blankets woven by the Chilkat was unique (see page 44). Other tribes excelled at basketry. The Nootka and Haida, for example, wove spruce tree roots into hats and strips of cedar bark into baskets. To add color, they stained grasses with fruit and plant dyes, then wove them into the finished basketwork.

PLAINS PAINTING

The creative skills of the nomadic Plains tribes were displayed for all to see on their tepees. Each family designed and painted its own tepee. Some chose to show events from their lives, such as hunting scenes or battles, while others preferred symbols intended to ward off evil. Geometric designs were also painted onto carrying cases called parfleches.

The people of the Plains excelled at quillwork and featherwork. Dyed porcupine quills were used to decorate everything from cradleboards to quivers for arrows. The feathers of golden eagles and other birds of prey were used for warbonnets and shields. Golden eagles were considered sacred, so men were not allowed to shoot them with arrows. Instead they had to kill them with their bare hands before plucking out the feathers.

Women of the Plains tribes made parfleches by folding buffalo hides. This case was used to carry dried buffalo meat.

These Plains moccasins are finely decorated with porcupine quills.

PUEBLO POTTERY

Pottery was made from the earliest times in the Southwestern Pueblos, and at the time of European invasion in the 16th century it was still a widespread skill held by women only. Women made pots by coiling a roll of clay higher and higher, then rubbing the surface until the joints between the layers were smoothed away. They then painted the finished pots in the traditional colors of red, black, and white. Some pots were used for everyday purposes such as storing food and water, but others played a part in sacred ceremonies. Zuni prayer bowls, for example, were filled with cornmeal then carried during rituals designed to bring rain.

The Pueblo peoples were expert weavers, producing garments from cotton and baskets from plants such as reeds. They were also skilled

A CLOSER LOOK

The Apache and Navajo learned many of their skills from the Pueblo peoples, only developing their own distinctive wool-weaving techniques after contact with Europeans. During religious rituals, the Navajo also made sand paintings. These were pictures of the spirits made from sand, cornmeal, pollen, and charcoal. Their purpose was to encourage the spirits to do what the people wanted, for example to cure the sick.

Navajo weavers at work.

A CLOSER LOOK
After the arrival of Europeans, Native Americans incorporated European styles, techniques, and materials into their creations. In particular, many tribes began to use glass beads bought from Europeans for decorating clothes, cradleboards, quivers, and other items, instead of traditional porcupine quills. Some tribes also adopted European embroidery techniques taught to them by missionaries.

woodworkers and creative jewelers. They could paint, too, decorating the walls of their underground kivas with sacred and secret images.

SOUTHEASTERN SKILLS

One of the main crafts of the Southeast was basketry. Women from tribes such as the Cherokee dyed reed stems a variety of different colors, then wove them into baskets featuring geometric patterns. Women also made clay pots that were not painted, but covered in surface indentations. These were created by carving the design required onto a small wooden tool, then pressing this repeatedly over the pots.

A colorful Pomo basket, with hummingbird and other feathers worked into the weave.

WESTERN ARTS

In the Great Basin and the High Plateau country, basketry was developed to a high level. Intricately woven baskets featuring complex designs and several colors were produced in many different styles. Among the most common were large, cone-shaped containers used for carrying food plants. But it was the Pomo of California who were the supreme basketmakers of the West. They often used several materials, such as reeds, roots, and bark, to form the basic framework of a basket, then wove hummingbird and other feathers into the design. The results were both stunning and unique.

A FINAL NOTE

Christopher Columbus never set foot on North American soil. On the four voyages he made between 1492 and 1504, he visited only some Caribbean islands and the coasts of South and Central America. Nevertheless, his arrival was a major turning point in world history, and opened the way for Europeans to explore – and colonize – all the Americas. These lands were never to be the same again.

SPANISH ENCOUNTERS

It was the Spanish who made the first major explorations of North America, looking for gold and whatever else might make them rich. Between 1539 and 1542, Hernando de Soto and his men covered a vast area of the Southeast, beginning in what is now Florida and continuing as far as Texas. His treatment of the Native Americans was a sign of what was to come in many other parts of the continent. As he passed from one settlement to the next, he required

This 16th-century illustration shows Native Americans of Florida preparing a feast. Hernando de Soto would have witnessed scenes such as this as he made his way across the Southeast.

people to submit to him and convert to Christianity. If they refused to do so, he stole their goods, put them in chains, and made them slaves. A similar story unfolded when Francisco Vásquez de Coronado encountered the Pueblo peoples of the Southwest in 1542.

The Spanish eventually colonized Florida in 1565. By 1700 they controlled much of the Southwest and were attempting to spread their way of life among its inhabitants. Their efforts to continue farther up the west coast were hampered by Russians, who also laid claim to the land.

FRENCH EXPLORATION

Farther north, it was the French who began to venture inland and meet Native American tribes. Frenchman Jacques Cartier arrived in Canada in 1534 and made his final voyage there in 1542. During his visits he came into contact with members of the Micmac, Huron, and other tribes, and established friendly relations with them. This soon led to the growth of trade in beaver, mink, and other furs, which Native Americans caught and sold to Europeans.

Later French explorers began to claim North American land for France. In 1608, Samuel de Champlain founded and claimed Quebec, and in 1682, René Sieur de la Salle declared the whole of the Mississippi Valley a French possession. He called it Louisiana after Louis XIV. By 1700, the French had control of a great strip of land across the middle of the North American continent.

ENGLISH COLONIZATION

The first English attempts at colonization of North America were not made until the late 16th century, and it was only in 1606 that the first successful settlement was founded, in Jamestown, Virginia. There, the new arrivals clashed with the local Powhatan tribe and nearly wiped them out in 1644.

Meanwhile in 1620, Puritan settlers known as the

Pilgrims had arrived farther to the north in what is now Massachusetts. They owed their survival to the Wampanoags and other tribes of the region, who taught them how to fish, hunt, and grow crops in their new environment. However, as the settlers grew more successful, they tried to take over more land. When the Native Americans resisted, the English attacked the Wampanoag and their allies. Soon the tribe that had once helped the colonists almost ceased to exist. By 1700, the English had colonized much of the East Coast.

THE ROAD TO THE RESERVATIONS

By the 19th century, many Native American tribes had been destroyed or forced to adopt European ways of life. However, the Plains tribes in the center of the country had managed to survive. The

This painting on buffalo hide was made by members of the Shoshone tribe. It depicts a buffalo dance, a ceremony often carried out immediately before or after a hunt. During the 19th century, both these features of Plains Indian life came to an end following the deliberate slaughter of millions of buffalo (see page 58).

A CLOSER LOOK
Europeans gradually devastated the ancient ways of life of the Native American peoples. Besides killing them in battle, they forced many others from their homelands. They also introduced European diseases such as measles, influenza, tuberculosis, and smallpox. The Native Americans had never encountered these diseases before and had no natural immunity to them. As a result, thousands of Native Americans died.

introduction of horses and guns by Europeans, and the arrival of new tribes who had been driven from their original lands, had greatly changed their ways of life. But they still lived by hunting buffalo and maintained many of their old traditions. Then, in mid-century, the situation began to change.

From the late 1840s, increasing numbers of Europeans began to head west, some in search of gold, others wanting land to farm. The territories of the Plains peoples lay on their route. In 1851 the U.S. government adopted a policy of "concentration." This meant that each Plains tribe was concentrated in one area and was not permitted to venture beyond its boundaries. The tribes refused to keep these new rules but were unable to stop the flood of Europeans who now began to enter their lands.

Soon a long series of wars began between government forces and the Native Americans whose lands they were attempting to take by force. At the same time, the government paid professional hunters to slaughter the buffalo on which the Plains tribes depended. Each year from 1872 to 1874, three million buffalo were killed. In 1876, the Native Americans scored a major victory when they killed General Custer and his troops at the Battle of Little

A CLOSER LOOK

As the colonists became increasingly greedy for land, more and more Native American tribes were driven from their homelands. Usually the Native Americans were forced on to land that was far less fertile or desirable than their traditional territories. In the 1830s, the American government forced the Southeastern tribes from their territories. Their new "home" was to be Indian Territory, now the state of Oklahoma, farther to the west. The move began in 1831 and, by 1838, the Seminoles, Chickasaw, Choctaw, and Creek had made the journey, many dying from hunger and disease on the way. But the Cherokee refused to comply with the government's demands. So government soldiers forced them out and they embarked on what has become known as the "Trail of Tears," a journey of 800 miles (1,300 km). Of the 13,000 Native Americans who set out, only 9,000 arrived at their destination.

Bighorn. But this was only a reprieve. The end finally came at the Massacre of Wounded Knee on December 29, 1890, when the Dakota leader Big Foot and 200 of his people were slaughtered by American soldiers. As a result, the Native Americans were forced to accept government demands and move to the lands that had been set aside for them, known as reservations.

SPIRIT OF RENEWAL

A young girl in tribal dress at a powwow symbolizes the revival of Native American ways of life in the present-day U.S.

Since this tragic time, Native Americans have fought hard to regain their freedom and to rebuild their old ways of life. They are beginning to revive their ancient beliefs, skills, and languages, and there is even a move to reintroduce buffalo to the Plains. This spirit of renewal is expressed particularly in the powwow ceremonies that are held regularly in many parts of North America. Originally the name given to a tribal meeting accompanied by feasting and present-giving, the term has come to mean a social gathering at which Native Americans from many tribes meet, wear traditional costumes, perform traditional dances, and make traditional music.

A CLOSER LOOK

In the U.S. today, there are over 30 Native American "tribal" colleges. These colleges teach the skills necessary to be successful in the modern American world as well as ensuring the survival of ancient traditions and skills. Religious ceremonies are practiced and languages spoken and taught, allowing Native American culture to flourish.

TIMELINE

c. **60,000 years ago**	Beringia land bridge first emerges.
c. **40,000-12,000 years ago**	Waves of hunters cross from Siberia to Alaska on foot.
c. **40,000-10,000 years ago**	Paleo-Indian Period
B.C.	
c. **10,000-9200**	Period of the Clovis culture
c. **9000-8000**	Period of the Folsom culture
c. **8000**	Beginning of Archaic Period
c. **1000**	Early settlements of the Adena culture established in the Southeast.
	Dorset culture arises in the eastern Arctic.
Various dates from	
c. **1000**	Beginning of the Woodland Period—Native Americans practice agriculture.
c. **300**	Hopewell culture replaces Adena in the Southeast.
	Hohokam culture emerges in the Southwest.
c. **200**	Basketmakers emerge in the Southwest.
A.D.	
c. **3rd century**	Mogollon culture emerges in the Southwest.
c. **500**	Decline of Hopewell culture begins.
c. **700**	Mississippians emerge in the Southeast. Anasazi emerge in the Southwest.
c. **1000**	Thule culture develops in Alaska. Mogollon begin to live above ground.
c. **1050-1250**	Mississippian town of Cahokia at its height
c. **1100**	Anasazi begin to build cliffside apartment houses.
c. **1300**	Hohokam begin to construct adobe villages.
14th century	Decline of the Mogollon culture. Anasazi abandon their villages.
c. **1450**	Decline of Mississippians begins. Decline of Hohokam culture begins.
15th century	Apache and Navajo tribes arrive in the Southwest.
1492-1504	Christopher Columbus's voyages to the Americas
1534-42	Jacques Cartier makes three voyages to Canada.
1539-42	Hernando de Soto crosses the Southeast.
1540-2	Francisco Vásquez de Coronado crosses the Southwest.
1565	The Spanish colonize Florida.
Late 16th century	Mohawk, Onondaga, Seneca, Oneida, and Cayuga tribes form the Iroquois League.
1606	First successful English colony founded in Jamestown, Virginia.
1608	Samuel de Champlain founds Quebec.
1620	Puritan settlers from England
1682	René Sieur de la Salle claims the Mississippi River Valley for France and names it Louisiana.
18th century	Southeastern Creek tribe moves to Florida and becomes the Seminole.
1840s	Europeans begin to head for the American West in large numbers.
1850s-1890	Wars between Native Americans and forces of the U.S. government
1851	The U.S. government confines each Plains tribe to a fixed area.
1870-1883	Extermination of the Plains buffalo herds by professional hunters
1876	Native Americans defeat General Custer at the Battle of Little Bighorn.
1890	Big Foot and about 200 other Dakota killed by U.S. government troops at the Massacre of Wounded Knee.

GLOSSARY

adobe – brick made of sun-dried mud.
anthropologist – a person who studies human beings and their ways of life.
archaeologist – a person who studies the past by excavating ancient sites and examining ancient objects.
chickee – an open-sided house of Florida's Seminole tribe.
corral – an enclosed area into which animals are driven and captured.
cradleboard – a lace-up leather pouch with a wooden back in which Native American women carried their babies.
culture area – one of the ten areas into which anthropologists divide North America. The Native American tribes in each area often have similar ways of life.
earth lodge – a sunken, dome-shaped dwelling of earth, wood, and grass, inhabited by the farming tribes of the Plains.
earthwork – a large, raised structure made of earth.
gourd – any of several types of fruit with thick, often brightly colored shells.
hierarchical – arranged in ranks or classes.
hogan – a wood-and-earth dwelling with a domed roof.
hunter-gatherer – a person who acquires food by hunting animals and gathering plants.
Ice Age – any of several periods of Earth's history during which much of the planet's surface was covered with ice. The most recent Ice Age lasted from about 1.6 million to about 11,000 years ago.
kachina – one of the many spirits recognized by the Pueblo peoples of the Southwest.
kayak – a type of small, wood-and-sealskin canoe used by Arctic tribes.
kiva – an underground room used for religious rituals by men of the Pueblo peoples.
longhouse – a large, rectangular, wood-and-bark dwelling with a curved roof inhabited by members of some Northeastern tribes.

mastodon – any of a group of extinct, elephantlike creatures with trunks and tusks.
midden – a garbage mound.
moccasin – a type of shoe made from soft leather and worn by tribes from several culture areas, including the Subarctic and Northeast.
moiety – one of two groups to which the clans of some Northwestern tribes belonged.
parfleche – a carrying case used by Plains tribes and made by folding buffalo hides into a box or envelope shape.
potlatch – a ceremony held by Northwestern tribes at which large numbers of gifts were distributed by the host.
powwow – a tribal meeting, now often a mainly social event with dancing, music-making, etc.
rawhide – an animal skin with hair removed but not treated to turn it into leather.
shaman – a man or woman believed to have the ability to contact the spirits and use their power, for example to heal the sick.
stockade – a fence or other barrier made of wooden stakes.
tepee – a tentlike dwelling made of buffalo hides stretched over wooden poles.
totem – any of several spirit animals, such as a bear or an eagle, that each symbolized a different Northwestern clan or moiety.
travois – a triangular wood-and-buffalo hide frame drawn by a dog or horse and used to transport goods.
tuber – a thick, underground stem.
tundra – the treeless area of permanently frozen ground between the Arctic ice cap and the forested region further south.
umiak – a type of sailing boat made of wood or whalebone covered with walrus hides and used by Arctic tribes.
wampum – valuable shell beads used by Northeastern tribes to create objects such as belts. After the arrival of Europeans, wampum became a form of currency.
wickiup – a cone-shaped dwelling made of wood and brush.

FURTHER READING

Bendix, Jane. *Mi'Ca: Buffalo Hunter.* Council for Indian Education, 1992

Beyer. *Indians of the Totem Pole.* Childrens, 1991

Clark, Ella. *Guardian Spirit Quest,* "Indian Culture Series." Council for Indian Education, 1974

Finley, Carol. *Art of the Far North: Inuit Sculpture, Drawing, and Printmaking,* "Art Around the World" series. Lerner, 1998

Lee. *Seminoles.* Childrens, 1991

Levin, Beatrice. *John Hawk: Seminole Saga,* "Council for Indian Education" series. Rinehart, 1994

Mails, Thomas E. *Spirits of the Plains,* "Library of Native Peoples" series. Council Oak Books, 1997

Olin, Caroline and Dutton, Bertha P. *Southwest Indians,* Book 1: (Navaho, Pima, Apache). Bellerophon Books, 1978

Porter, Dr. Frank W., general editor. "Indians of North America" series, including "Native Americans of the Southwest," "Native Americans of the Southeast," "Native Americans of the Great Plains," "Native Americans of the Northwest,"etc. Chelsea House, 1996

Shuter, Jane. *Francis Parkman and the Plains Indians,* "History Eyewitness" series, Raintree Steck-Vaughn, 1995

Warren, Scott S. *Cities in the Sand: The Ancient Civilizations of the Southwest.* Chronicle Books, 1992

INDEX